WE THE PEOPLE
CHAMPLAIN

Published by Creative Education, Inc. 123 South Broad Street, Mankato, Minnesota 56001

Copyright © 1988 by Creative Education, Inc. International copyrights reserved in all countries. No part of this book may be reproduced in any form without written permission from the publisher. Printed in the United States.

Library of Congress Cataloging-in-Publication Data

Zadra, Dan.
  Champlain ; explorer of New France (1567-1635)

  (We the people)
  Summary: A biography of the French explorer who founded Quebec, discovered Lake Champlain, and was called the Father of New France.
  1. Champlain, Samuel de, 1567-1635—Juvenile literature.   2. New France—Discovery and exploration—Juvenile literature.   3. Explorers—America—Biography—Juvenile literature.   4. Explorers—France—Biography—Juvenile literature.   5. America—Discovery and exploration—French—Juvenile literature.   [1. Champlain, Samuel de, 1567-1635.   2. Explorers.   3. New France—Discovery and exploration]   I. Henriksen, Harold, ill. II. Title.   III. Series: We the people (Mankato, Minn.)
  F1030.1.Z33   1988   973.1'8'0924   [B]   [92]   87-36393
  ISBN 0-88682-181-9

WE
THE PEOPLE
CHAMPLAIN

EXPLORER OF NEW FRANCE
(1567-1635)

DAN ZADRA

Illustrated By Harold Henriksen

CREATIVE EDUCATION

*WE
THE PEOPLE*
CHAMPLAIN

Eastern Canada was a wild, untamed land when the Vikings first sailed to her shores a thousand years ago. The Vikings were the first Europeans to see the craggy coastlines, beautiful bays and spectacular forests. But the Indians chased them away, and another 500 years went by.

The first white settlers came to stay in eastern Canada in the 16th Century. It wasn't land, lumber or gold that drew them to the New World. They came instead to harvest millions of pounds of tasty codfish from the frigid Atlantic. The fish were dried, salted and shipped to market in England, Portugal, Spain and France.

Soon, more and more fishermen came to Canada. Sometimes they traded with the red men—whom the French called the savages. Sometimes they looked for the Northwest Passage to China. And sometimes they sought the legendary land of Saguenay, where gold and jewels were supposed to lie in heaps.

One Frenchman, Jacques Cartier, claimed the Canadian mainland for his King in the year 1534. Cartier named the place New France. The French tried to start colonies. But the winters were too long, and the Indians were too hostile.

More than sixty years went by. During this time, neither France nor England cared very much about Canada. It remained a mysterious and beautiful land—unmapped and unwanted. It was good for fishing and fur-trading, but not much else.

Then, about 1570, a boy was born to a sea captain and his wife in Brouage, France. The boy's name was Samuel Champlain. He was destined to play an exciting role in the exploration of the New World—especially Canada.

From the time Samuel was very small, he sailed with his father and uncle. He learned to tie knots, mend sails, read the stars, and chart a course. By working very hard, he also learned the secrets of an extraordi-

nary trade—the making of maps.

From 1594 to 1598, Champlain was a quartermaster in the French army. France and England fought Spain—and won. Then Champlain had a chance to sail to the New World. He visited the wild West Indies, Mexico and Panama.

It was in Panama that Champlain had a wonderful idea. "Perhaps," he thought, "a passage could be found across the narrow Isthmus of Panama. If so, ships could reach the South Pacific in a few days rather than weeks." Champlain may have been the first map-maker to imagine what would one day become the great Panama Canal!

When he got back to France in 1601, Champlain wrote a report

about his adventures for King Henry IV. The King showed the report to some important men who were about to start a new French colony in North America. They invited Champlain to come with them and be the "official reporter" of the expedition.

On March 15, 1603, three ships sailed from France. After nearly two months of dodging icebergs and storms, they arrived in Canada—the New France.

They would sail boldly up the mighty St. Lawrence River to the roaring Lachine Rapids. First, they stopped at a summer trading post at Tadoussac. There, the Montagnais Indians surrounded them. But the French Captain had brought a special surprise for them. Aboard the ship

was a member of the tribe who had been kidnapped years before and taken to Europe. Now, the French had brought the Indian home as a gesture of peace.

With the Indians as guides, Champlain continued up the St. Lawrence in a small boat. He passed the site of today's Quebec City. Jacques Cartier's men had built a fort there in 1535, but it was in ruins.

Cartier had seen great villages along the river, but now they were gone. Probably, there had been an Indian war. Champlain did not worry about it. He mapped the river country as far upstream as the site of Montreal.

The Indians gave him good information on the country upstream. But its exploration would have to wait. The river was blocked by the great rapids above Montreal.

Well-satisfied, Champlain took his maps and returned to Tadoussac.

The fleet loaded up with codfish and furs. They sailed back to France in September, 1603.

Champlain wrote a book. He gave it a long title: *About the Savages, or, The Voyage Samuel Champlain Made to New France*. Today, that book is very valuable to historians because it describes in detail how the Canadian Indians lived their lives.

Encouraged by Champlain's discoveries, the King of France decided to colonize Canada. The King asked a nobleman, the Sieur de Monts, to set up a trading company. The company would bring settlers to New France. In return, it was given the fur trade for ten years.

Champlain became De Monts' second-in-command. He picked out

a townsite—not on the St. Lawrence, but in Acadia (now New Brunswick). Sailing up and down the coast, he mapped the country and made friends with the Indians. Unlike many Europeans, Champlain firmly believed that the red men deserved to be treated with honor. He respected Indian customs, so the local chiefs helped him to explore.

The French had hoped to find gold mines in Acadia. But there was only a little copper. They stayed in Acadia from 1604 to 1607, then went back to France. Champlain had explored the coast as far south as Cape Cod, Massachusetts.

In 1608, Champlain sailed from France for the fourth time. By now, he had become the official lieutenant governor of New France. On July 3, he founded Quebec—the first important European settlement in Canada.

Champlain knew that trade depended on friendship with the Montagnais, Algonkin, and Huron Indians who lived in New France. He agreed to help them in their war against the fierce Iroquois tribes of New York.

In 1609, Champlain led an Indian army to the lake that now bears his name. There was a battle and Champlain shot three enemy Mohawk chiefs. Frightened by the gunfire, the Mohawks fled.

The legend of Champlain was growing. He continued to explore and to build good relations with the Indians. He returned to Europe in

1610 and married Helene Boulle. But he was soon called back to New France on yet another expedition. This time he built an important trading station at Montreal.

In 1613, Champlain went up the Ottawa River by canoe. He braved dangerous waterfalls and rapids. The Indians were amazed that Champlain survived.

The Canadian Indians insisted that Champlain help them make war against the Iroquois. He went all the way to Lake Huron to pick up a war party. Then he went to New York's Lake Oneida, where he fought on the side of the Canadian Indians in a war with the Onondagas.

By taking sides in this Indian war, Champlain unwittingly caused great

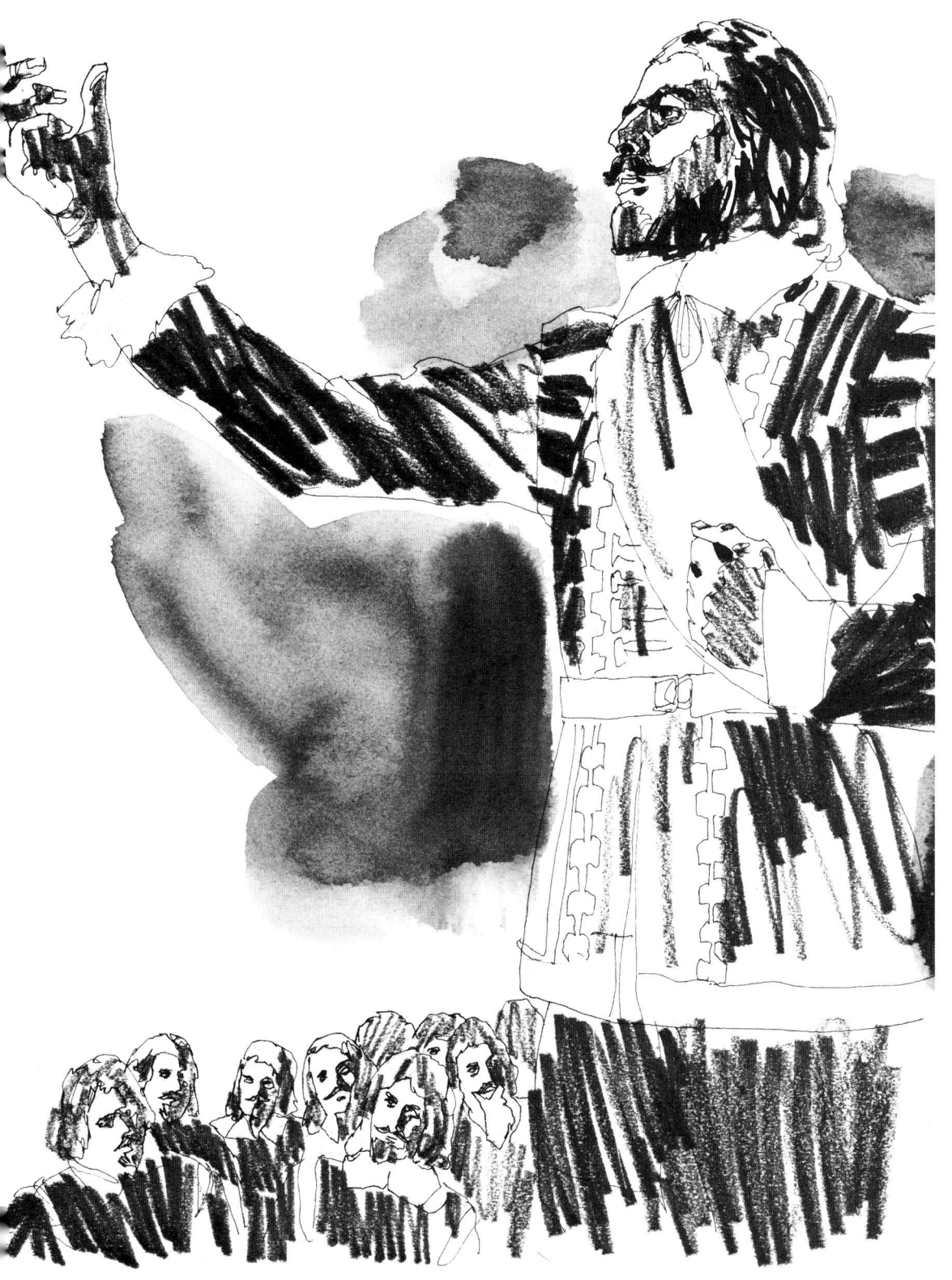

trouble for French settlers in the years to come.

Champlain had been wounded in the Battle of Onondaga. He spent the winter with the Indians. He became convinced that more French settlers were needed to help the Indians. That way, New France could someday become as civilized as France itself.

Champlain returned to France in 1616. There, he spoke out boldly on behalf of the New World. He warned the King that France would have to send more settlers to Canada or else the English might take the country. But the greedy French fur-merchants opposed settlement. They were afraid of competition.

But Champlain's dream would

not die. He persisted in asking for colonists. To set an example, he and his wife went to Quebec in 1620. Soon, however, she grew weary of the wilderness. The little town of Quebec was so remote and cold. Months would go by without any sign of food, clothing or medical supplies from France. So grim was life in frontier Canada that Helene finally decided to return to Europe in 1624. It was a sad day indeed for Samuel Champlain.

In 1629, the thing Champlain had feared most finally happened. England and France were at war and British ships captured Quebec. Champlain was taken to England where he was held prisoner until 1632. Fortunately, when the war ended, France was able to buy back Canada from the British.

Champlain became governor of New France in 1633.

For the rest of his life, he devoted himself to governing the colony. He was tireless in his efforts to convince the French King to help colonists. With his help, Quebec thrived. His wise policy of friendship toward the Indians promoted peace in Canada.

Samuel de Champlain—the Father of New France—died at his beloved Quebec on December 25, 1635. Almost single-handedly he had insured the life of France's colony in the New World.

WE THE PEOPLE SERIES

WOMEN OF AMERICA

CLARA BARTON
JANE ADDAMS
ELIZABETH BLACKWELL
HARRIET TUBMAN
SUSAN B. ANTHONY
DOLLEY MADISON

INDIANS OF AMERICA

GERONIMO
CRAZY HORSE
CHIEF JOSEPH
PONTIAC
SQUANTO
OSCEOLA

FRONTIERSMEN OF AMERICA

DANIEL BOONE
BUFFALO BILL
JIM BRIDGER
FRANCIS MARION
DAVY CROCKETT
KIT CARSON

WAR HEROES OF AMERICA

JOHN PAUL JONES
PAUL REVERE
ROBERT E. LEE
ULYSSES S. GRANT
SAM HOUSTON
LAFAYETTE

EXPLORERS OF AMERICA

COLUMBUS
LEIF ERICSON
DeSOTO
LEWIS AND CLARK
CHAMPLAIN
CORONADO